Edwin Cone Bissell

The Pentateuchal Analysis and Inspiration

Edwin Cone Bissell

The Pentateuchal Analysis and Inspiration

ISBN/EAN: 9783337180614

Printed in Europe, USA, Canada, Australia, Japan

Cover: Foto ©Lupo / pixelio.de

More available books at **www.hansebooks.com**

THE

HARTFORD SEMINARY RECORD

ISSUED UNDER THE AUSPICES OF

THE FACULTY

OF

Hartford Theological Seminary

PUBLISHED BI-MONTHLY

VOL. II. NO. 1 — OCTOBER. 1891

CONTENTS

PAGE

[Entered at the Hartford Post-Office as Second Class Matter]

HARTFORD, CONN.

1891

Hartford Seminary Record.

SPECIAL OFFERS.

A Complete set of the issues of Vol. I will be sent to any address (post-paid) for 50 cents. These issues contain, with other important matter,

Articles by President Hartranft on

BREADTH OF THOUGHT.

By E. H. Byington, on

OPEN-AIR PREACHING.

By Professor Zenos, on

INSPIRATION AND INERRANCY, Etc.

Also a Complete Alumni Register of the Seminary; also Editorials on Current Topics, numerous Book Reviews, Personal Items, Letters, Etc.

WE will bind up sets of Vol. I (if in good condition) at the following advantageous rates: Half-leather, 75 cents; Cloth, 50 cents. (Expenses of transportation to and from Hartford to be borne by the sender.)

Volume II will be sent to any address (post-paid) for $1.00.

Address orders to

THE RECORD,

Theological Seminary,
Hartford, Conn.

HARTFORD THEOLOGICAL SEMINARY.

Founded 1834.

FACULTY.

CHESTER D. HARTRANFT, D.D., PRESIDENT, Waldo Professor of Biblical and Ecclesiastical History, and Instructor in Encyclopædia and Methodology.

EDWIN C. BISSELL, D.D., Nettleton Professor of the Hebrew Language and Literature, and Instructor in Syriac and Biblical Aramaic.

GRAHAM TAYLOR, D.D., Samuel Hawes Professor of Practical Theology.

WALDO S. PRATT, A.M., Professor of Ecclesiastical Music and Hymnology, and Instructor in Elocution.

MELANCTHON W. JACOBUS, A.M., Hosmer Professor of New Testament Exegesis.

CLARK S. BEARDSLEE, A.M., Associate Professor of Systematic Theology.

WILLISTON WALKER, PH. D., Associate Professor of Ecclesiastical History.

ARTHUR L. GILLETT, A.M., Associate Professor of Apologetics.

ALFRED T. PERRY, A.M., Instructor in Bibliology, and Librarian.

AUGUSTUS C. THOMPSON, D.D., Lecturer on Foreign Missions.

AUSTIN B. BASSETT, B.D., Lecturer on Experiential Theology.

CHARLES C. STEARNS, A.M., Carew Lecturer for 1891-92. Subject: "New Lights from Old Records of a Forgotten People."

The Bible holds a central position in the system of the institution. The course of study aims (1) to establish sound methods of *investigating* the Scriptures, (2) to train the power of *formulating* Scriptural truth, and (3) to indicate the way of *applying* that truth to the facts of history and experience and to all problems of the present and the future. Hence, the Seminary presents God's thought and God's will as the supreme objects of all science and the supreme guides of all conduct. It is thus forced to oppose all rationalistic and secularizing tendencies. Its chief purpose as an educational agency is the formation under God of personal religious character, as the only basis for scholarship, conduct, and power.

The method of instruction is partly through text-books, partly by lectures, and partly through original investigation on the part of the student. Emphasis is laid throughout upon a close personal relation between instructor and pupil. The apparatus includes ample buildings, a library of 45,000 volumes and over 20,000 pamphlets, reading-room, gymnasium, etc. Methods believed to be peculiarly effective are used in Hebrew and Greek, in history, in dogmatic theology, and in pastoral theology. In the latter field extensive practical work is expected in preaching, in the methods of all varieties of evangelistic and charitable effort, and in personal Christian work. Systematic instruction is given in music and elocution. In view of the value to students of theology of a knowledge of German, instruction in that language is provided. With the present year a large part of the course becomes elective.

Special and advanced courses are provided for those who desire them.

Four prizes and two fellowships for foreign study, are offered.

TERMS OF ADMISSION.— Candidates for admission must be members of some Christian church and graduates of some college (or at least of sufficient literary acquisition to undertake the regular course). Those who are not college graduates may be admitted *on probation* during the first semester.

All courses are open to *women* on the same terms as to men.

EXPENSES.— No charge is made for tuition, rooms, furniture and bedding, or use of the library and apparatus, except a nominal fee of $20 for use of steam and for supervision. Board is provided at the Seminary under the care of the Students' Association, at $3.50 per week.

Scholarship aid is provided for those needing it to the amount of $60 to $100 per year, in addition to the grant of $75 from the Education Society.

CALENDAR.— The fifty-eighth year begins on Sept. 17, 1891, and closes on May 12, 1892. The various courses are arranged in two semesters, the second of which begins on Jan. 18, 1892. Examinations are held at the close of both semesters.

For the annual Register, address either the PRESIDENT or the REGISTRAR.

CYCLING FOR CLERGYMEN.

■ ■ ■ ■ ■

IT is now a well-established fact that the bicycle is a practical machine for ministers. It affords them the best of exercise ; it takes them to the farthest bounds of a large parish with ease and speed ; it keeps them in touch with the young men and women ; and costs less than a horse.

TESTIMONIALS.

There is no better tonic for a man who must think and study much, and whose habits must be therefore sedentary, than a spin upon the wheel.—*Rev. Wayland Hoyt, Philadelphia, Pa.*

I am not given to public testimonials. This is my first one. But the bicycle [Columbia] has been such a benefit to me as a Minister of the Gospel that, unsolicited, I desire to recommend it to my fellow-ministers. It does for the nervous system all that horseback riding supplies, and with but a trifle of the expense. I would not be without one.—*Rev. M. W. Lisle, Pastor of Stewart Street Baptist Church, Providence, R. I.*

I have ridden a bicycle for four seasons, and if some one should offer to give me the best horse in the country and pay for his keeping, on the condition that I should never ride the bicycle again, I should, without hesitation, refuse the offer.—*Rev. Charles E. Stowe, Hartford, Conn.*

From my use of a cycle for the past three years, I can conscientiously say that it is the best mode of exercise, and the most healthful means of real pleasure that I can obtain, and that any one can desire.—*Rev. Robert Granger, Rector St. John's Church, Richfield Springs, N. Y.*

COLUMBIA CYCLES

Catalogue Free.

Highest Grade Only.

POPE MANUFACTURING CO.,

77 FRANKLIN STREET, BOSTON, MASS.

Factory, Hartford, Conn.

BRANCH HOUSES:

12 Warren St., NEW YORK.   291 Wabash Ave., CHICAGO.

HARTFORD SEMINARY PUBLICATIONS.

1. **Some Thoughts on the Scope of Theology and Theological Education.** By PRESIDENT CHESTER D. HARTRANFT. May, 1888. 24 pp. [*Price, 10 cents.*]

2. **The Practical Training Needed for the Ministry of To-Day.** By PROFESSOR GRAHAM TAYLOR. October, 1888. 19 pp. [*Price, 10 cents.*]

3. **The Relations of New Testament Study to the Present Age.** By PROFESSOR ANDREW C. ZENOS. January, 1889. 19 pp. [*Price, 10 cents.*]

7-8. **Studies in the English Bible and Suggestions about Methods of Christian Work.** By PROFESSORS CLARK S. BEARDSLEE and GRAHAM TAYLOR. A practical help for pastors, lay-workers, Bible-classes, the Y. M. C. A., Christian Endeavor Societies, etc. Eight numbers, 25-30 pp. each. December, 1889, to July, 1890. [*Price, 50 cents for the entire set. Liberal discount on orders of more than ten copies.*] These STUDIES and SUGGESTIONS have been widely used in all parts of the United States and Canada.

9. **The Nature of Public Worship.** By PROFESSOR WALDO S. PRATT. January, 1890. 24 pp. [*Price, 10 cents.*]

10. **A Religious Census of the City of Hartford.** Being a reprint of a Report of the Connecticut Bible Society. The canvass and the tabulations are principally the work of Seminary students, working under the direction of PROFESSOR GRAHAM TAYLOR. February, 1890. 40 pp. [*Price, 20 cents.*]

12. **A Hebrew Vocabulary of the Psalms.** By ARTHUR S. FISKE. (Thompson Fellow.) Adapted in size to Baer & Delitzsch's edition of the Psalms. First issued in 1887. 42 pp. [*Price, 30 cents.*]

For copies of the above, address the REGISTRAR.

HARTFORD STEAM BOILER

INSPECTION AND INSURANCE CO.

ORGANIZED 1866

THOROUGH INSPECTIONS

AND

Insurance against loss or damage to property
and loss of life and injury to
persons caused by

STEAM BOILER EXPLOSIONS.

J. M. ALLEN, President.　　　W. B. FRANKLIN, Vice-Prest.
J. B. PIERCE, Secy.　　　F. B. ALLEN, 2d Vice-Prest.

THE

HARTFORD SEMINARY RECORD

Vol. II. No. 1 — October, 1891

Published bi-monthly on the 15th of October, December, February, April, June, and August. Subscription price, $1.00 per year, in advance. Remit to order of THE RECORD, Theological Seminary, Hartford, Conn.

WITH THIS number the RECORD enters upon its second volume. The general plan and aim of the magazine remain as heretofore. While seeking to act primarily as a medium of intercommunication among the constituency of Hartford Theological Seminary, we shall continue to discuss topics of general interest by means of editorial notes, articles, and book reviews. We have made arrangements to devote most of the space at our disposal for contributed articles to the discussion of the questions of Biblical inspiration and authority, and of their practical applications, which are so much engaging the thought of American Christians as of their brethren over sea. The studies which we shall present are all prepared especially for our pages and will be the work of specialists. In accordance with this plan, Professor Bissell in this number states and illustrates some of the bearings of Pentateuchal criticism, as conducted in certain quarters, upon the commonly received doctrine of the inspiration of the Scriptures. The writer's acknowledged position as an authority gives great weight to his views as here presented.

THE AIR of popular discussion is full, apparently as never before, of talk about the Bible. What is the Bible? In what sense is it the Word of God? Is it sufficient? Is it infallible?

Is it supreme? These and similar searching questions are to be heard on every hand, urgently pressed, often by confessed unbelievers, as if they had never been asked before. We do not at all share the alarm that some good people feel about the bluntness with which these and similar questions are sometimes asked; though we admit that bluntness may be heedless and brutal as well as earnest. We rather welcome serious inquiry about these vital subjects, both because it betokens a real interest on the questioner's part, and because it forces the Christian believer to give reasons both to himself and to others for the faith that is in him. The net results of such questioning, — setting aside those cases in which it is plainly insincere and flippant, — in the long run can only be good. Truth is truth, and the more of it that is fully ascertained and firmly seated in the popular mind by means of persistent inquiry and discussion, the better.

OUR LEADING demominational newspaper devoted a large part of one of its recent issues to a statistical and critical study of the facts of Sunday observance, occupation, and travel in and around the city of Boston on the first Sunday of August. Decided skill was displayed both in commissioning competent reporters and in properly combining their reports into a consecutive, well balanced, and readable statement. We are impressed, however, not so much by the journalistic enterprise and ability which this effort showed, as by the illustration it afforded of a most essential prerequisite in systematic religious work, namely, an energetic gathering of the facts of the field under consideration. When we compare the methods of parish analysis and investigation of too many of our really earnest workers (not to speak of the entire lack of such methods among half-hearted ones) with the check-lists of the politicians, the personal visitations of the assessors, the police, and other municipal officials, and even the peripatetic inquiries of book-canvassers and plant-venders, — when we contrast the aimless and wholly inaccurate study of many parishes for religious purposes with these and other persistent investigations, we must confess that "the sons of the light" are not only apparently but really far behind "the sons of this world." Aggressive Christian work, whatever its particular field, cannot be intelligently done without a mastery of the actual topography, population, customs, and peculiar circumstances of its field. We welcome every attempt, by whomsoever made, to provide such preliminary material. We rejoice, for instance, in the capital studies of the Connecticut Bible Society. We applaud the growing habit of making parish censuses, registers, and maps. We thoroughly endorse the house-to-house canvasses of the Evangelical Alliance. And we trust that soon such investigations will be going on from so many centers that a network of interlacing religious investigations will cover the whole face of the land. Thus only can a sure basis be provided for sound evangelistic progress. Toward this basis every pastor, every church, every religious organization, and newspaper should be contributing constantly and systematically.

THE STATEMENT that the Bible should occupy a central position in thought and education, without distinction of secular and religious, conveys very different impressions to different minds. To some, it seems to threaten a return to the intellectual follies of the middle ages. The school-men held as their favorite maxim that all other learning was but the handmaid of theology. If the Bible be made central in all thought, in all science, will it not be necessary to forsake the inductive method, and return to *à priori* reasoning? No man in his right mind would advocate deserting the inductive method, but the placing of the Bible in this position of supremacy involves no such return to mediæval methods. To make the Bible central, or rather to make Biblical theology central, in all thought and in all education is simply to include the most important of all facts in the inductions we make. We plead for an extension of the inductive method, rather than for a limitation or desertion of its use.

Again, others suppose that the placing of the Bible in the position suggested involves the acceptance of certain theories of its composition or method. Yet certainly one need not accept anything more than the doctrinal infallibility of Scripture to be obliged by his very belief to urge the placing of the Bible in the position which this infallibility gives it the right to hold. He may believe that Moses wrote the Pentateuch, or he may contend that its present form cannot be older than the age of Ezra; he may accept the existence of two authors of the prophecy of Isaiah, or may be able to see no sufficient evidence that there was more than one; he may maintain most strongly that no mistake as to fact is to be found within the covers of the Bible, or he may consider its historical statements as no more credible than those of other books. His firm belief is that the truth has been revealed by God to the prophets and apostles, and that they have been inspired, in a way the student is perhaps not ready to define, to record the revelations which have been vouchsafed to them.

The belief we hold is simply this: that in studying nature, which has been made by God; in studying philosophy, which is false if it does not result in a correct appreciation of God's character and purposes; in studying the conditions and problems of human society, which is struggling, however blindly, toward a God-appointed ideal, it is worse than foolish, it is absolutely destructive of correctness in method and conclusion, to refuse to give the central place in our thinking to the revelation of God's thoughts which He has given in the Bible. That the adoption of such a belief involves a radical change in the methods of theological and general education, we admit, and even assert. We have no fear of successful contradiction in declaring that the present methods of education demand renewing. There is an unrest among educators greater than that among theologians, almost as great as that among the laboring men. May it not be that the satisfaction of theologian, of educator, and of laborer alike is to come through acceptance of the supremacy of the Scriptures in thought, and obedience to its teachings in life? It surely can come in no other way which has yet been suggested.

WE ARE glad to announce that in our next issue we shall give one more installment of Mr. Byington's unique discussion of Open-Air Preaching.

THE PENTATEUCHAL ANALYSIS AND INSPIRATION.

The opinion is very commonly expressed that whether the new theories respecting Pentateuchal analysis prevail or not, the matter of the divine inspiration and authority of the Bible will be little, if at all, affected. So distinguished a scholar, for instance, as Cheyne, pronounces the results of all the later biblical criticism "harmless," — harmless, that is, if they are accepted. " Harmless, I call them," he says, "not insignificant ; they mean reform as an alternative to revolution." * Prof. Driver writes to the same effect : "It is a mistake to imagine, as is sometimes done, that the critical view of the formation of the Pentateuch is framed in the interests of unbelief, or has its foundation in the premises of a negative theology. Particular critics may indeed share these premises and employ arguments which the present writer, for instance, would repudiate ; but the grounds upon which in fact the critical position depends are neutral theologically, and consist simply of the application to a particular case of the canons and principles by which evidence is estimated and history judged."† In the *Presbyterian Review* for April, 1887, Prof. Briggs wrote: "Whoever in these times, in the discussion of the literary phenomena of the Hexateuch, appeals to the ignorance and prejudices of the multitude as if there were any peril to the faith in these processes of the Higher Criticism risks his reputation for scholarship by so doing." Prof. S. I. Curtiss, in a recent article in the *Independent* (July 30) says : "If we accept the views of modern critics regarding the origin of the Old Testament as correct so far as the evidence may seem overwhelming, we do not thereby rob the Scriptures of their divine character."

It will be found, however, that persons who speak in this way, if, like those just quoted, they know what they are talking about, either tacitly or expressly modify for themselves the ordinary epithets applied to the Bible, using them in a sense, it would appear, not yet current in our churches. So it is with

* *Contemp. Rev.*, Aug., 1889, p. 221.
† *Critical Notes on the Internat. S. S. Lessons*, New York, 1887.

Driver, who adds in the context of the passage quoted from him :
"We are bound, indeed, as Christians, to accept the authority
of the Old Testament, and to see in it a divine preparation
for the revelation of Jesus Christ made in the Gospels; but
there is no obligation upon us to accept a specific theory [*i. e.*,
the ordinary one], either of its literary structure or of the
course of history which it narrates. . . . The fact of revelation
will not be affected ; we shall only have modified our view —
perhaps have obtained a truer view of the form in which it was
manifested, or of the course along which it advanced." Prof.
Curtiss, likewise, wishes distinctly to be understood as rever-
ently maintaining that "all Scripture is given by inspiration of
God," and that interpreted by the principles of the Gospel, "it
is the only infallible rule of faith and practice." He holds,
according to an editorial in the number of the *Independent* suc-
ceeding the one above quoted, "most firmly to the divine
character of Scripture as something which cannot be overthrown by any established results of criticism or scientific
investigation. So far as historical errors or imperfect ethics
and doctrine may appear in the Old Testament, he maintains
that this appertains to the human side of Scripture, because
God in His divine wisdom did not deem it necessary in making
a revelation that there should be anything more than an honest
attempt to transmit the facts of history ; and in the character
of Old Testament ethics and doctrine God has had respect to
the weaknesses and limitations of men who were not prepared
for the high demands of the New Testament." *

Such explanations and disclaimers, however, when made —
they are unfortunately more frequently omitted — are generally
overlooked by readers, or fail to have the force they were
intended to have. In any case they fall far short of giving an
adequate impression of the extent to which current views of
the inspiration and inerrancy of the Bible will need to be
changed if the proposed analysis of the Pentateuch is adopted
on the grounds proposed. A hint at the true state of the case
is given by Prof. W. R. Harper in connection with a paper in
Hebraica.† Among other similar things, he says : "If there is
an analysis, the sacred record can no longer be claimed to pre-

* *Independent*, July 30, 1891.
† Oct., 1888, pp. 68-70.

sent a perfectly accurate account of these early times ; for conflicting accounts stand side by side ; changes have been arbitrarily introduced into the text ; insertions and omissions have been made ; the material cannot be called in a strict sense historical." Again, he says : " If there be an analysis there are two, though, perhaps, not contradictory, conceptions of God, one of which seems to border closely on polytheism. How is it possible for so low (this is the proper term) an idea of God to have been incorporated in the sacred Scriptures ? " And he adds still further : " If all this is true, the character of the Old Testament material, whether viewed (a) from an archæological, (b) from an historical, and especially (c) from a religious point of view, must be estimated somewhat differently from the method commonly in vogue. It is composed of different stories of the same event, joined together by an editor who did not have insight sufficient to enable him to see that he was all the time committing grave blunders, and yet felt no hesitancy in altering the originals with which he was working ; it is not historical in the ordinary sense of the word."

Without proposing directly to call in question here the correctness and sufficiency of the grounds on which the current Pentateuchal analysis rests, I wish to show in this paper what, in the nature of things, some of its effects must be on the ordinary view of biblical inspiration ; in other words, to point out more definitely and in detail what Prof. Harper has so frankly admitted in a general way. I would call attention, first, to the *wholesale and intentional falsification* which it presupposes. The material is too abundant to be treated otherwise than by example. Let us look at the work of the so-called Redactor in Genesis. According to the theory, that book was made up from three principal documents or original histories (J., P., and E.), widely separated in origin, and considerably degenerated in form from long circulating independently, the first two appearing mainly in chapters 1–20, and the three intermingled in the remaining chapters. The work of the Redactor was mostly compilation. His unique method in this respect will be considered later ; we will look now at his more original work.

In 7: 3, 9, 23,* the account of the Deluge, there are

---

* I follow the analysis of Kautzsch and Socin, *Die Genesis, etc.*, 2te Aufl., Freiburg, 1891.

three instances where he inserts in one of his authorities words taken from, or only suitable to the other in (what has proven) a futile attempt at harmony in two irreconcilable documents. Other efforts to smooth over abrupt transitions, or to supply additional information by the insertion of extraneous matter appear in 9: 18, 19; 10: 9, 16, 18, 24. In 12: 17, he has without authority added the words "and his house." In 13: 1, he has likewise altered the documentary record by inserting "and Lot with him." In 15: 7, 8, 12–16, 19–21, he has introduced a large amount of matter into what was originally a simple account of a sacrifice by Abraham, giving a wholly different meaning to the transaction. In 16: 8–10, there is another attempt at harmonizing conflicting statements by supplying words which are put into the mouths of Hagar and of Jehovah. In 17: 10, there is a similar insertion of unauthorized material, and here, in what purports to be a direct promise from God to Abraham. In 21: 1 and in 22: 11 he has changed the word *Elohim* to *Jehovah*. In the latter chapter he is also responsible for verses 14–18, *i. e.*, for the important promises of Jehovah to Abraham and the naming of the place where he offered Isaac, "Jehovah-jireh." In verse 20 he is guilty of a gross chronological misstatement by putting in the words, "after these things," which, if real, belong elsewhere and to another document. In 24: 67, he has deliberately inserted the misleading words "his mother" and "his mother Sarah." In 26: 1, he asserts what he must have known to be untrue, that the famine there described was a different one from that which occurred in the days of Abraham ; and the context contains three other falsifications of the record (verses 2–5, 15, 18). To make a smoother transition between chapters 27 and 28, and give an appearance of continuity, he forged verse 27 of the former. In place of "Laban" he put in "Jacob" in 31 : 45. Again, to give the appearance of a continuous narrative where there was, in fact, merely a two-fold account of the same event, he inserted the word "again" in 35 : 9. Throughout the history of Joseph (37: 5, 8, 10; 39: 1, 8, 20, 23; 42: 7, 28: 43: 14; 45: 19–21; 46: 1, 3, 5, 8–27; 47: 4, 24; 48: 7, 21; 49: 28; 50: 22), he did apparently his best by arbitrary insertions, changing proper names, transferring matter from one source to

9

another, and other, as from the basis of the theory must be
allowed, unwarrantable alterations to produce from his threefold
originals of the one story a pleasing verisimilitude which
should pass for truth.

But is not this a harsh and unfair judgment touching this
ancient editor? May he not rather have been inspired to do
this work and may not the combination he has effected, supposing
it to be actual, be the very truth we are to believe? By no
means. That is the precise thing which the criticism, if it has
proven anything, has shown to be impossible. It is claimed as
one of its highest triumphs that it has succeeded in tracing
this man's blind and tortuous methods. It is the documents
which he manipulated that contain whatever of truth really
existed in the early records. To find out what that truth is
other tests are needful. We must, it is said, apply to each particular case "the canons and principles by which evidence is
estimated, and history judged" (Driver, as quoted above).

That this process is not as easy as might be supposed has been
sufficiently shown in another periodical by Dr. Green, who says: *
"These documents give, it is claimed, not only varying but
mutually inconsistent accounts of the persons and events which
they describe, and this not only in subordinate and unessential
particulars, but in matters of the greatest moment. And they
have been put together in such a manner as to give an entirely
different complexion to things from that which either of the
documents taken singly aimed to give. Their incompatible
statements have been harmonized in an unwarrantable manner,
and their divergent accounts of the same event have been con-
verted into distinct events, showing that the redactor misun-
derstood or misrepresented his sources. His misconceptions
would have been of less consequence if he had preserved the
documents entire and unaltered, so that adequate means would
have been possessed for forming an independent judgment of
their contents. But, on the showing of the critics themselves,
the documents have been preserved in a mutilated form, that
only being retained by the redactor which seemed to him suited
to his purpose; and this was often modified considerably from
its original intent by the new connections in which it was
placed; and certain passages were besides seriously altered or

2

additions made which still further obscure the genuine significa-
tion. So that he who would arrive at the real truth respecting
the matters treated in the Pentateuch, must first ascertain and
expunge what has been inserted by the redactor, and restore
what he has changed to its previous form. He must then dis-
cover and correct the modifications to which the documents
have been subjected in the various editions through which they
are severally alleged to have passed. When this task has been
successfully accomplished, and what is left of the documents
has been restored in each case to its primitive form, these will
put the investigator in possession of all that now remains of
the traditions which were circulating about the Mosaic age six
or more centuries subsequently. From these mutually contradictory legends he must evolve the facts. And this is the sort
of voucher we have for the revelations made to Moses, and the
institutions founded by him, which are the basis of the Old
Testament religion and the foundation on which the New Testament likewise rests."

In connection with the remaining four books of the Pentateuch attention will be called to the Redactor's * special effort
to make his work seem ancient, in fact, Mosaic. In Ex. – Num.
we will illustrate the point exclusively from the document known
as P.†. Its age is variously conjectured, a smaller circle of critics
placing it somewhat earlier than Deuteronomy (B. C. 621), but
most much later, dating it, in its completed form, subsequent
to the exile (B. C. 444). Only extremists among them hold to
actual, at least literal and formal, Mosaic history and legislation
in this source. To all outward appearance, however, as we shall
see, this is quite otherwise.

For example, there is the law concerning blasphemy (Lev.
24: 15, 16; Num. 15 : 30, 31); not only does it purport to be
the outcome of an event of the Mosaic history (Lev. 24 : 10 –
14), but to have been given by Jehovah directly through Moses.
Elsewhere an entire chapter (Ex. 28) is devoted to a description of the priestly vestments. They are "for Aaron and

---

* For the purposes of this paper it is immaterial whether the editorial supervision of the
Pentateuch was in the hands of one person, or of many ; it is simply the nature and spirit of
such supervision that we are considering.

† The same three documents noted above are alleged to be at the basis of the first four
books of the Bible.

his sons," and it is Moses who is represented as making the necessary provision for them. To render the deception more complete the Urim and Thummim are introduced, the existence and
use of which are never heard of after Abiathar or David's time,
five hundred years before the exile. So the consecration of the
priests (Ex. 29 : 1–22), the preparation of the anointing oil
(Ex. 30 : 22–33), the law for the ordinary priests (Lev. 10 : 8–11;
21 : 1–24), and that for the succession of the high priest
(Num. 25 : 10–13) are all in the most explicit manner said to
have been mediated by Moses. Aaron, who is most directly
concerned, is also there, but only as a secondary figure even in
these priestly matters. Moses is not only put into the history
in an extraordinary manner, supposing him to have no right
there, but he is made to dominate it, voicing everywhere the
divine authority during the exodus period. He determined who
should eat of the sacrifices (Lev. 22 : 1–16 ; Num. 18 : 10 ff.),
prescribed not only the duties, but the prerogatives of the priest-
hood (Num. 6 : 22–27 ; 10 : 1–10), and laid down the long list
of regulations under which the tabernacle was constructed and
used (Ex. chaps. 25–27 ; 36–38).

In short, every law contained in Leviticus and the first ten
chapters of Numbers, besides the great mass of the others
contained in the middle books of the Pentateuch, are represented as having been given during the period intervening
between the setting up of the Tabernacle and the departure
from Sinai ; that is, under the immediate supervision of Moses
(with Ex. 40 : 17 ; cf. Num. 10 : 11). There is not the slightest
hesitation on the part of leading critics in acknowledging
even more than this. For example, Kuenen says : * "On
the face of the whole legislation, of course, we‧read that
the theatre is *the desert ;* Israel is encamped there ; the
settlement in Canaan is in the future. With regard to the
laws in Ex. xxv, *sqq. ;* Lev. i, *sqq.;* Num. iv, *sqq.;* xix., etc.,
this is elaborately shown to be the case by Bleek ("Einl.," p.
29, *sqq. ;* 4th ed.), but it is also applicable in the main to Ex.
xxi—xxiii (see especially xxiii, 20, *sqq.*), and to Deuteronomy.
In other words, it is not only the superscriptions that assign
the laws to Moses, and locate them in the desert, but the form
of the legislation likewise accords with this determination of

---

* *The Hexateuch,* p. 25.

time and place. . . . The representation given in the Hexateuch of the legislative activity of Moses involves *the essential
unity of the Tora.* . . . There can be no question, therefore, that if we place ourselves at the point of view of the Hexateuch itself, we are justified in regarding the ordinances of
Exodus — Deuteronomy as *the several parts of a single body of
legislation,* and comparing them with one another as such."

For this uniformly antique coloring, however, given to matter, dating all the way from David to Nehemiah, the Redactor
alone is responsible. With whatever intent — our critics are not
wanting in charitable judgment here — he simply masquerades
in the name and supposable character of Moses and his contemporaries. To say nothing of the conception of such a character
as Moses on the part of the Redactor, the conception of such
a character as the Redactor on the part of our critics, we may
remark in passing, is something surprising. So plumply, so
boldly, and with such consummate art does he present the matter
that not only did he succeed in duping the latest generations of
men until now, but left no trace of the fraud he perpetrated on
the history or traditions of his times. On the contrary, he
seemed to the people then, and seems to those instructed in
New Testament models, to have moved on the very highest
moral uplands. He has made universally the impression of
being governed by a moral and religious purpose so grand and
pure that it has never been excelled. Nevertheless his ostensi-
ble statement of facts, it is said, cannot be accepted. Indeed,
to all human appearance, he would have contributed vastly
more to the cause of truth and the reign of righteousness, if he
had left the laws he communicated without their "stolen livery"
of a bygone age.

Again, the "consensus of criticism" has assigned the book
of Deuteronomy to the period of King Josiah (B. C. 621), or
about eight hundred years after Moses.* It is unnecessary to
say that its claim to Mosaic origin is stamped on its every page.

* "Two points at least ought, I think, by the most skeptically inclined critic to be accepted as historical, viz.: (1) that the 'law-book' was published in Josiah's reign with the view
of recommending certain reforms and establishing the national religion on a firmer basis; (2)
that Hilkiah, one of its chief promulgators, asserted that he had found it in the temple. The
view implied (probably) in 2 Kings xxii., and expressed in 2 Chronicles xxxiv., that the
'book of *Torah*' had the leader of the Exodus for its author, cannot from a critical point of
view be maintained, for these, among other reasons, that the Deuteronomist (if we may so for

The book opens with the announcement: " These be the words which Moses spake unto all Israel beyond Jordan," the place and time being indicated with extreme exactitude. The great lawgiver's name occurs thirty-seven times in the composition, and, generally, with the aim of connecting him authoritatively with its contents. As matter of fact, almost the entire book is represented as uttered directly by him, he being left everywhere to speak *in propria personâ.* He is even made responsible for the literary form of the work after giving the substance of it as an address, being declared to have written it "to the end " (31 : 9) and, subsequently, to have committed it to the custody of the Levites (31 : 24). He is depicted, moreover, as addressing himself to his hearers as though they had been actual contemporaries of the actual Moses. " We saw," he says, " the sons of the Anakim " (1 : 28) ; again, " In the wilderness thou didst see how the Lord did bare thee as a man doth bear his son " (1 : 31); and again, " The Lord thy God will raise up unto thee a prophet from the midst of thee, of thy brethren, like unto me " (18 : 15). Here, too, we shall be pardoned for calling attention to the extraordinary art, if it be such, of this ancient writer (Hilkiah ?). The subtle coloring of the book is wholly of the Mosaic age. There is no hint of such a city as Jerusalem, although a principal purpose of its author was to emphasize the centralization of worship. The great empire of Assyria, already dominant for hundreds of years, casts not the slightest shadow of itself on his page ; while the freshest reminiscences of Egypt are scattered thickly about. There are nearly twoscore references to it by name. The boldness and freedom of the author, too, are worthy of attention. He knows the story of the Exodus ; but he is independent of it, shaping the rich material in a way altogether his own. He dares to put his hand upon the sacred code of Sinai, and even that central portion and glory of it which was written in stone by the finger of God, assuming the right to give it an altered form. He could not have presumed upon more, if he had really been the original law-giver. And with how nice a tact he leaves Moses several

convenience refer to the author or joint-authors of the original Deuteronomy) has (1) employed documents manifestly later than Moses, (2) made allusion to circumstances which only existed long after Moses, and (3) expressed ideas which are not such as are, psychologically speaking, possible in the age of Moses." Cheyne, *Jeremiah : His Life and Times,* p. 90.

times to speak of his desire to enter the promised land : "I must die," he says, " in this land. I may not go over Jordan. But ye will go over to possess that good land " (4 : 22 ; 7 : 23–29) ; and does not hesitate even to make conspicuous the good man's serious lapse at Meribah (4 : 21 : *cf.* Num. 20 : 10) in order to cover up more completely his own identity.

Admitting that the book of Deuteronomy was the product of the age of King Josiah, it does appear not a little strange that such *extraordinary*, and, as it might be thought, *disproportionate and largely unnecessary* means were made to impute it to Moses. Would not a tithe of the effort have been even more effective? But that is not now the question ; rather, how much the Spirit of God can have had to do with the conception and execution of such a work. Are Deuteronomy and its companion books inspired? And in what sense and degree are they inspired? A definition of inspiration widely current is this : " It is that divine influence which, accompanying the sacred writers equally in all they wrote, secured the infallible truth of their writings in every part, both in idea and expression, and determined the selection and distribution of their material according to the divine purpose." * It is clear enough that, if the analysis is to be adopted, such a definition will answer no longer ; and that Prof. Harper has put the facts altogether too mildly when he says : " If all this be true, the character of the Old Testament . . . must be estimated *somewhat differently* from the method commonly in vogue." The lamented Dr. Dwinell comes nearer the truth: " The only inspiration possible under this theory is of a very equivocal order, morally and spiritually ; for it is an inspiration that does not keep the sacred writers from making up a pretended framework of history in which to set their characters and instructions. It does not interfere with their asserting things to be facts which never took place. It does not stand in the way of consciously antedating and representing things as having occurred centuries before which really occurred later, or of deliberately writing after the events had taken place, and giving the writing the form of prediction and passing it off as prophecy. It does not stay the sacred authors from writing out of their own intuitions or experience or thoughts and reasonings, and claiming

* Hodge, *Outlines of Theology*, p. 67.

that these teachings came directly from God. A kind of inspiration which admits of all these duplicities and falsities must be accepted as true if this criticism is admitted. Surely inspiration drops down to a low and ignominious plane on this theory! No wonder there is a cry all over the world from those who follow the critics that the doctrine of inspiration must be recast! Yes, *down-cast!*" *

But let us, secondly, glance at the material itself with which the Redactor had to do, the original documents from which he is supposed to have compiled. If his peculiar manipulation of them, as cursorily described, has an important bearing on the doctrine of inspiration, his alleged sources have a much more important bearing. If that shows "wholesale and intentional falsification," these will show, we are quite sure, *an almost innumerable list of contradictions and a wholly indescribable confusion of thought in the opening books of the Bible.†*

To begin at the beginning, there are two radically distinct accounts of the Creation (Gen. 1–2 : 4^a ; 2 : 4^b–23), resulting from the juxtaposition of the two principal documents of Genesis. One, P, represents the creation as proceeding from lower to higher forms of life ; J, the reverse ; in P there is too much water for vegetation; in J, too little ; in P man and woman were created together; in J the order is man, vegetation, animals, woman ; in P man is given supreme authority over the earth at once ; in J he attains it only after sin and punishment ; in P man is created in God's image to rule over the earth ; in J it is a sin for man to seek to be as God, to know the world ; in P the universe is conceived of as a "diving-bell" in water ; in J the earth is an indefinite extent of dry plain on which the water must be poured by Jehovah. P is monotheistic, avoids the anthropomorphic terms of J, exalts God far above man, attributes to him especially power and benevolence, presents a progressive revelation culminating in the Sabbath ; while J does not so rigidly exhibit monotheism, represents that God's rights may be invaded by man, that the work of creation is hardly from an infinite being, but a sort of demi-god, that man is on

---

* *Moses and His Recent Critics,* Funk & Wagnalls, pp. 307, 308.

† Any one desiring to see a definite scheme of the analysis and the arguments by which it is supported from the hands of competent American scholars should consult *Hebraica* (The Student Publishing Co., Hartford), from October, 1887.

free and even confidential terms with God, capable himself of gaining superhuman authority. Now, among many, one of the most serious aspects of the case in this view of it is that the weaker and more mythical document is the one that contains what has been supposed to be the supremely important narrative of the fall and the promise of man's recovery (Gen. 3 : 1-14). And if it be true, as Prof. Harper states, that its view of God "borders closely on polytheism," is but "slightly removed from paganism," and that it must dispute the claim of being in any degree true with its far more recent and better supported neighbor, what theory of inspiration must be adopted in order to get the assurance of special divine authority for it ?

The supposed history contained in chapters four and five of Genesis is to be similarly decomposed and precipitated by the chemical tests of the criticism before a proper estimate can be formed of its value. There are two distinct and variously discrepant narratives covering the same ground (J : chap. 4, except 16ᵇ-24 ; P : chap. 5, except verse 28, "a son," and verse 29). The genealogies, though represented in the text as showing different lines, are really the same thing in different forms. By some blunder they have become attached to different ancestors. Here, too, the document J appears extremely weak compared with its neighbor. Its anthropomorphisms are, as usual, excessive. It makes Jehovah assist at child-birth, have a heated discussion with Cain, represents that Cain should have had more knowledge than he exhibits concerning sacrifice. Contrary to P, it would make out that public worship, feasts, and sacrifices were common at this early period, while the latter places them much later.

The narrative of the Flood (Gen., chaps. 6-9), is said to show in a marked degree evidence of the combination of duplicate accounts. According to P, the beginning of the flood is dated by the life of Noah (7 : 6, 11, 13) ; the flood is caused by convulsions of nature ; the waters prevail one hundred and fifty days ; they disappear and the earth is dry after two months (8 : 13ᵃ, 14). According to J the flood is announced but seven days before its appearance (7 : 4, 10) ; the rain was on the earth forty days and nights ; the ground dries up after one hundred and one days (8 : 6, 8, 10, 12, 13ᵇ). P's ark has a window system and a door in the side ; J's has a window and a cover. J's distinction between clean and unclean animals is foreign to P. J makes the flood local and limited ; P, universal. In theology the difference is the same as before. J looks upon the Deity as a sort of demigod, who can have familiar intercourse with men. He speaks of altars and sacrifices, etc., while P regards them as first beginning with Moses. These supposed duplicates, as is sufficiently plain from the examples given of their differences, are totally irreconcilable with one another. The fact of the flood is vouched for, indeed, by both ; but for the details of it, it will require a master of historical research to tell us where the truth lies, especially amid the maze of similar stories outside the Bible.*

So throughout the biblical account of the Patriarchs there is the same duplication of material and dubiety of impression, until we come to the twentieth chapter of Genesis, when the confusion is increased by the use of a new document containing still another version of the events narrated. Did Abraham have any quarrels in his family or not (Abraham with Lot, Sarah with Hagar)? Did Sarah actually go down with him into Egypt? The associated authorities differ on these points. Can circumcision be dated from Abraham's time? It might be thought of some importance theologically ; but the document J, which is much the older, knows nothing of it. The facts concerning Hagar and Ishmael are particularly muddled by the two accounts. By one, Ishmael being unborn, Hagar is so treated that she flees ; by the other, she is driven out with the child on her shoulder.† By one, Hagar is at fault ; by the other, it is Ishmael. The record, moreover, is inconsistent in representing that Ishmael is carried on the shoulder at all ; since he is too old to be so treated (P and J, 16 : 1–16, except 8–10–R ; E 21 : 8–21). The representation of a two-fold covenant with Abraham (chaps. 15 and 17) is likewise false. It is the same event twice described, and the differences, which are by no means few, it is necessary to charge, as so often before, to the account of profit and loss.

---

* Cf. Preface to Rabbi Wise's excellent work just issued : "God only did create light out of darkness ; man cannot produce truth out of fiction, unless in his self-delusion problematic truth satisfies him. All so called gems of truth buried under the quicksand of fiction and deception are problematic, at best, if not supported by authoritative corroborants. None can speak conscientiously of Bible truth before he knows that the Bible is true, and especially in its historical data." *Pronaos to Holy Writ*, Cincinnati, 1891.

† The text of the LXX. is followed.

The double, and sometimes triple, reason given for proper names, as that of Ishmael (J 16:11, 12; P 17:18, 21), of Isaac (P 17:17; J 18:12; E 21:6), of Edom (J 25:25; 25:30) of several of Jacob's sons, of Mahanaim, Penuel, and of Israel (J 32:25-32; P 35:10) though it is assumed that only one of them can be correct, might be considered trifling discrepancies. Can the same be said of the representation that Isaac and Rebecca's adventure with Abimelech was original with them, when it was only a revamping of Abraham and Sarah's under similar circumstances; of the contradictory statements about the maid of Rebecca (J 24:59; E 35:8); Jacob's sons (J E 35:16-18; P 35:23-26); Rachel's death (J E 35:19; E 37:10); how Joseph came to be in Egypt, one account stating that he was "stolen"; the other that he was "sold," etc., etc., to the end of Genesis and the end of the Hexateuch?

For let it not be forgotten that this method of composition, if true anywhere, is true throughout; and the documentary theory as elaborated by our critics applies no less to the middle books of the Pentateuch and to Joshua than to Genesis. There is no pretense of establishing the three codes of laws, dating, severally, B. C. 1000, 621, 444, except as based on the showing that in a multitude of particulars they are in irreconcilable contradiction with one another as products of the Mosaic age. There is as little concealment of methods as of results in the principal critical treatises of our times. This is as it should be. The only ground for surprise is that with the really tremendous change of attitude towards the Bible, necessitated by this treatment of it, Christian scholars who are fully aware of this change should speak of it as "harmless," as theologically "neutral" in its effects; should say that any one who thinks there is "peril to the faith in these processes of the Higher Criticism risks his reputation for scholarship" thereby, and is still able to use, unmodified, the old formula that "all Scripture is given by inspiration of God." Undoubtedly these expressions are quite sincerely made. Our sole contention is that the words "Scripture" and "inspiration" as thus used have never as yet been naturalized among us.

What are just now seriously needed are clear ideas and all the facts on this most important subject. There would appear to be complete confusion in the public mind, as represented in platform and press, as to the real nature and reach of the critical questions involved. The writer of this paper would be the last one to raise a bar to the freest and fullest investigation of the Scriptures by critics high or low. He has no sympathy whatever with that vehement and mostly indiscriminate denunciation of them which is coming to be altogether too common. He believes that much good will result from these discussions, especially if they can be conducted with mutual respect and forbearance. He not only holds without abatement or mental reservation, and "most firmly, to the divine character of the Scriptures as something which cannot be overthrown," but, essentially, still, to the old theory of their origin, not excepting the Pentateuch. He does not hesitate to say that, in his judgment, not hastily or superficially formed, the arguments used by German critics and their followers for the analysis of the latter are demonstrably fallacious, and hence wholly inadequate to prove the theories based upon them ; and that, in no long time, they will be abandoned by their authors themselves.

But none of these matters come directly within the purview of this article. Its one object is to serve, in some measure, to disabuse the public mind — which seems to have become somewhat dangerously charged with the contrary sentiment — of the idea that Pentateuchal analysis as conducted by our critics is a sort of "harmless" by-play and amusement of theirs, scarcely concerning the ordinary Christian ; a purely "literary question," involving no serious doctrines of the Christian faith. Within the narrow limits allowed us in this magazine, it was only possible to present a bare specimen of the grave results which are inevitable if it be established. An important series of specifications touching the Messianic Hope* and the changes which will be necessary in the ordinary view of the relations between the Old and New Testaments has been wholly omitted.

It is said, indeed, that one is carefully to distinguish between the analysis of our critics, and the conclusions which

---

* What value remains, for instance, to the so-called Protevangelium (Gen. 3:15) the tap-root of all subsequent Messianic prophecy ; of the subsequent promise to Abraham (Gen. 12:1-3) ; and, especially, of that notable prediction put into the mouth of Moses (Deut. 18:15), to which, as it is customary to suppose, our Lord directly referred in support of his claims (John 5: 46)?

they themselves make from it. True ; but it is not possible to accept the analysis without accepting, in their main features, the arguments which are used in its support. No attempt has been made, that we are aware of, to justify or defend the analysis on other grounds than those we have been considering, viz. : the general unreliability of the text of the Bible in its first five books, in which, along with not a little intangible legend, there is mixed up an almost inextricable mass of contradictions and misstatements. We are in fullest accord, therefore, with the judgment of Prof. W. H. Green, expressed in a recent article on a similar theme :* " It does not annul the inherently vicious character or the evil tendencies of this hypothesis that men revered for their learning and piety have of late signified their acceptance of it, and that they consider its adoption compatible with whatever is essential to the Christian faith. It is a remarkable phenomenon that in European universities eminent biblical scholarship has been to so great an extent dissociated from faith in the Scriptures in any evangelical sense. We may wisely employ the Philistines to sharpen our spears and our swords ; but we cannot join them in an assault upon the camp of Israel. No more perilous enterprise was ever attempted by men held in honor in the church than the wholesale commendation of the results of an unbelieving criticism in application both to the Pentateuch and to the rest of the Bible, as though they were the incontestable product of the highest scholarship. They who have been themselves thoroughly grounded in the Christian faith may, by a happy inconsistency, hold fast their old convictions while admitting principles, methods, and conclusions which are logically at war with them. But who can be surprised if others shall, with stricter logic, carry what has thus been commended to them to its legitimate issue?"

EDWIN CONE BISSELL.

* *Old Test. Student*, July 1887, p. 318.

Book Notes.

The Best Books. A reader's guide to the choice of the best available books (about 50,000) in every department of science, art, and literature, with the dates of the first and last editions, and the price, size, and publisher's name of each book. By William Swan Sonnenschein. 2d ed. London : Swan Sonnenschein & Co., New York : G. P. Putnam's Sons, 1891. pp. cix, 1,009.

The above work is excellently described by its title, an uncommon virtue to begin with, accompanied by the almost equally uncommon merits of wide and catholic inclusion, judicious selection, practical classification, and sensible condensed annotation.

The section on theology occupies pages 1–120, say 6,000 titles, classified under ten general heads and one hundred and twenty-four sub-heads. There is a full index of authors and titles. The classification is by no disciple of Dr. Hartranft, and the selection by no graduate of Hartford Seminary ; moreover, any bibliographer can doubtless pick flaws typographical and otherwise. (For example, Professor Bissell's initials are twice given as " C. C.") But it is a work which by its nature is to be judged on its positive side, and in this aspect any bibliographer, who examines carefully, must heartily declare its remarkable excellence, the product of extreme practical intelligence and industry. Its predecessors — Dowling, Malcolm, Hurst, Case — the various theological encyclopædias, and the like, have their own excellences, but this work is the first modern one which furnishes a real usable guide to primary theological literature.

The method and quality of the work may be illustrated by the following random samples : Three works by Dr. Bissell (described as " Am. Cong.") are included ; the *Apocrypha* annotated " An original work appended to Lange's commentary," the *Biblical Antiquities* annotated " Student's book," and the *Pentateuch* annotated " an interesting and thorough examination of recent theories."

The author mentions 27 works on the Pentateuch, annotating more or less 18 of them. On miracles he mentions 14, starring, as having special value, Bruce, Mozley, Steinmeyer, and Trench.

The book is too expensive for the ordinary theological student, but a copy or two in every theological library, checked by the various professors as to books really worth owning. and supplemented in the class rooms, would be invaluable to all who are forming theological libraries. [E. C. R.]

(21)

Romans Dissected. A Critical Analysis of the Epistle to the Romans. By E. D. McRealsham. Edinburgh: T. & T. Clark; New York: Charles Scribner's Sons, 1891. pp. 95.

This little book of ninety-five royal octavo pages appeared at nearly the same time in German (Erlangen and Leipzig), as in English. It was written as a travesty on current methods of Pentateuchal criticism, and there is no denying that it has hit the bull's-eye. The Epistle to the Romans is almost universally admitted to be a unit and a genuine production of Paul. But employing the devices of Pentateuchal critics without exaggeration, it is proven to be by four different writers, no one of whom was Paul.

A critical analysis of the epistle discloses different points of view. One writer (G', using the name of "God" for the Deity almost exclusively) makes salvation depend on obedience to the law. A second (G²) makes it depend on faith in God. A third (JC., using for the Deity the title "Jesus Christ") makes faith in Christ's vicarious death the chief thing. A fourth (CJ., who uses the title "Christ Jesus") shows that Christian life is a life in the Spirit, etc.

With the difference in the use of the divine names correspond not alone the difference in doctrinal teaching, but in style and language. The argument is entirely *à propos* and it is shown that if it have weight in the Pentateuch it must have special weight here.

In a fourth and final chapter the alleged "conflict between facts and theories" is considered. It is shown that the theory proposed relieves one of many difficulties; the indecisiveness of historical testimony is dwelt upon; and the facility of ancient writers in introducing forgeries. From various data it is concluded that G¹ wrote between A. D. 80 and 90; G² between 100 and 110; JC. between 115 and 125; and CJ. between 130 and 140. A Redactor brought together the writings about A. D. 150, and already, in A. D. 175, Irenaeus apparently regards the composite as a genuine work of Paul.

This book should be widely read. For a little book it is a good deal of a boomerang for the advocates of the current Pentateuchal analysis. [E. C. B.]

Syntax of the Moods and Tenses in New Testament Greek. By Ernest DeWitt Burton, Professor in Newton Theological Institution. Bartlett & Co., Boston, 1891. pp. 44.

This is a published issue of what was first a privately printed pamphlet for use in the author's classes. It does not aim to be exhaustive in its treatment, nor does it lay claim to any "high degree of originality" in what it presents. It is not intended for students of historical grammar — but simply for those who have studied classic Greek along the lines of Hadley or Goodwin and who wish now to be interpreters of the Greek New Testament and translators of it into English word and thought. It is practical, rather than technically scientific. We believe, therefore, that it must be service-able in the seminary class-room, though the student may feel he can not dispense with his Buttman or his Winer. And we are not at all surprised that, having tried it in his own work, the author now finds himself under the pleasant necessity of placing it before the public for general use.

We do not wish here to enter upon a discussion of the grammat-ical merits of the brochure. There is doubtless but little that would call for criticism. We would simply suggest that there is a more definite service yet that the author can render the New Testament student-class. And, as there is hinted in the announcement that "a revised and enlarged edition" of the pamphlet is likely to be issued within another year, we make bold to hope that the suggestion may possibly be carried out.

There is needed in seminary study a grammar that will keep step with the student as he reads. We understand of course that there are differences between the Greek of the Epistles and the Greek of the Gos-pels — between the Greek of the Synoptics and the Greek of John — between the Greek even of Luke and the Greek of his fellow Evangel-ists, Matthew and Mark — and we understand that these differences are in the sphere of grammar, as well as vocabulary and synonymy. Now it may not be within the author's purpose to enlarge his pamphlet to an outline of New Testament grammar. But, even should he keep along the confined lines that he has already marked out for himself, could he not, after he has given the student a summary of general rules, go with him into his Epistle and his Gospel and Acts exegesis, and specialize his valuable data, so that it shall be a complete and exhaustive help to the Tense and Mood study of each group of books — or, if he will, to each particular book by itself? We sin-cerely hope that this may be done.

The method of grammar teaching employed to-day is different from the method employed a dozen years ago. Its new teaching should be followed up into the seminary class-room. Such a work as we have suggested to the author we believe would be helpful to this end. [M. W. J.]

The Divine Order of Human Society. Being the L. P. Stone Lectures for 1891. Delivered in Princeton Theological Seminary. By Professor Robert Ellis Thompson, S.T.D., University of Pennsylvania. Philadelphia, John D. Wattles, 1891. pp. 274.

It is a rare privilege to welcome an avowedly and distinctively Christian treatise on the science of sociology. Appeals to and invocations of the Bible and its Gospel are notably frequent in current sociological literature, especially that of the communistic and socialistic order. But the power-literature of this science of many sciences is almost exclusively agnostic, or avowedly anti-Christian. Comte and Spencer are as yet by far the greatest names in the scientific literature of the subject. And they do not hesitate to declare any one who believes in a divine Providence thereby incapacitated for the study of sociology. Prevision being essential to this materialistic conception of all development, the admission of any volitional interposition, divine or human, is precluded *a priori*. It still remains to be seen how long the Christian Church will continue to ignore the apologetic, much more the practical, bearing of thus tacitly surrendering into the hands of materialistic evolutionists the formulation of the Science of Society, which has to do, not only theoretically, but constructively, with the three normal forms of all institutional life, the family, the state, and the Church itself.

But here is an author who, in full view of the wide range of sociological literature, "needs make no apology for beginning with the Bible," and for regarding it as the first source of a "higher sociology"; who maintains sociology to have been a science of evolution long before Darwin: who denies that progress and civilization are the outcome of unvarying "natural law" or that the savage is the normal man : and affirms the divine will and human freedom, the Incarnation and regeneration to be more primal and potent, constant and calculable forces in social development than heredity and environment. Profoundly convinced that the present truth — the truth demanded by the needs and the cravings of to-day — is the proclamation of the Kingdom of God, *i. e.*, the revelation of God to men in social relations and social duties, the Stone Lecturer for 1891 has very successfully accomplished the object of his course, namely, to put his hearers and readers into the right attitude to appreciate the broad outlines of Christian sociology, the significance of the problems of the family, the state, and the Church, and the bearings of proposed solutions. The foundations of our Christian lectureships can be invested in no way to yield a larger return to the Christianity of the future than in the production by such studies as these of a scientific Christian sociology.   [C. T.]

The Darkness and Daylight: or Lights and Shadows of New York Life. By Helen Campbell, Col. Thomas W. Knox, and Inspector Thomas Byrnes. A. D. Worthington & Co., Hartford, 1891. pp. xii, 740.

The weird and alarming echoes awakened by that "exceeding bitter" *Cry of Outcast London* continue to resound throughout the world. The same year that it was issued by the Congregational Union, George R. Sims published, with sixty illustrations, his awful description of *How the Poor Live.* Pamphlets on *Down in the Depths of Outcast London, One-Room Life in London, etc.,* rapidly followed. Then came W. T. Stead's heroic disclosures of the contribution of so-called higher life to the wickedness of the depths. In 1889, Charles Booth, assisted by a corps of seven other contributors, edited the most scientific analysis of the *Life and Labour of the People in East London* that has ever been made of any population. Out of that district itself came the Rev. and Mrs. S. A. Barnett's suggestive little volume on *Practicable Socialism.* Last, but by no means least, perhaps greater than all in its practical effect, arose the call to the people of England to do something to save the "submerged tenth," uttered by the General of the Salvation Army through that trumpet-voiced book, *In Darkest England and the Way Out.*

In this country Dr. Josiah Strong clearly led the way along this line of literature in convening an Inter-Denominational Congress in the interests of City Evangelization at Cincinnati in 1885, whose discussions are published by Cranston & Stowe. "Our Country" soon followed, and is yet to follow and to lead. Riis' *How the Other Half Lives* vividly portrays the condition of the poor in New York City, and especially the horrors of the tenement-house system. Well worthy to be classed with these epoch-making books in evangelistic and philanthropic literature is the subscription volume recently published in handsome form, with photographic illustrations, entitled *Darkness and Daylight of New York Life.* The "Darkness" is depicted as none could more grimly fathom it than Inspector Byrnes, Chief of the New York Police. The "Life" could hardly be more graphically reproduced than by the journalistic pen of Col. Thomas W. Knox, aided by flash-light photography. The "Daylight" is that of Christian city evangelism and philanthropy, which none know better how to describe than Mrs. Helen Campbell, author of *The Problem of the Poor,* and *Prisoners of Poverty,* and the correspondent of the New York *Tribune* on the social statistics of the depressed classes. [G. T.]

The Pacific. Vol. XL. Edited and Published by the Publishing Co. of The Pacific. San Francisco, Cal.

Congregational weeklies are now numerous from ocean to ocean, but when the *Pacific* was established in early California days it had no neighbor. It was a pioneer, has grown up with the country, and completes forty years of useful life the present month. The first impression on opening the *Pacific* is its admirable type and the familiar names of its contributors. Published in a great city and serving a region in itself an empire, its correspondence includes all the great centers of religious life east of the Rockies. No paper more truly cosmopolitan, in respect to its widely scattered contributors and the regions they represent, comes to our table. Its editorials are concise and timely, and both these and the news department have a genuine western avoidance of all circumlocution. The way the *Pacific* calls some sins by name and points them out to its readers is likely, if practiced with even-handed justice, to "throw a coldness" over its constituency, unless they are people in dead earnest to improve their hearts and lives at every cost. A man may be partially judged by his favorite books and newspapers. Our study of the *Pacific* enlarges and exalts our conception of the growing Congregational community to which it has so long ministered.

[F. S. H.]

The Presbyterian. Vol. LXI. Published by Mutchmore & Co., Philadelphia, Pa.

Few things bring home to the mind such a sense of the varieties of Christian thought and feeling among us as does the examination of the religious papers representing denominations other than one's own. Here is an excellent antidote for provincialism in religion. Would that all our ministers and laymen could take and read two religious newspapers, — the favorite denominational paper and a representative journal of another Christian fellowship.

"Revision" and kindred subjects now agitating the body represented by the *Presbyterian* occupy several columns in that journal. Other subjects are, however, widely represented, and the field of religious intelligence, foreign lands not excepted, is well covered. The editorials fill more than a fifth of the space, and are very generally colored by the condition of the Presbyterian Church of to-day. Earnest, strong, and free from bitterness, though dealing some severe blows, they are easily the first thing an intelligent subscriber would read. The *Presbyterian* is a low-priced weekly, but it ought to be printed upon better paper. The setting is wholly unworthy the contents.

[F. S. H.]

Alumni News.

The Western Massachusetts Alumni Association held its annual meeting, September 28, at Cooley's hotel in Springfield, with sessions in the morning and afternoon. The attendance was good, both active and corresponding members being well represented, and the Association receiving as its guests Professor Taylor, of the Seminary, and T. M. Hodgdon, '88, of West Hartford, on behalf of the Connecticut Association. There were also present several ladies from the Women's Advisory Committee of Springfield.

The morning session was chiefly occupied by business and informal discussion. In the absence of the President, C. S. Mills, '85, who had already gone to his new work in Cleveland, the chair was taken by the Vice-President, G. W. Winch, '75, of Holyoke, who was appointed President for the ensuing year. Other officers were elected as follows: Vice-President, A. B. Bassett, '87, of Ware; Secretary and Treasurer, E. H. Knight, '80, West Springfield; Executive Committee, the above officers and J. P. Harvey, '80, of Ware, and F. S. Hatch, '75, of Monson. Reports were made by the chairmen of the committees on Instruction and Apparatus and on Endowment, together with which informal statements were made concerning the working of the plan for the admission of women to the Seminary, and concerning the RECORD. By unanimous vote the Association expressed its hearty appreciation of the labors of the editors of the RECORD. The interest taken in these matters showed the advantage of having a place and time where the friends of the Seminary may informally, but freely and thoroughly, discuss all matters of current interest in relation to the practical working of the Seminary.

After a recess for dinner, which made a highly enjoyable social hour, the Association resumed its session for a discussion of the question, " Does the common curriculum in our theological seminaries need revision to meet the needs of the present age?" The discussion was opened by G. R. Hewitt, '86, of West Springfield, who gave illustrations from the different seminaries to show what the common

(27)

28

course is, and then proceeded to indicate how, in his opinion, this course should be modified, laying special stress upon the study of sociology as one of the great needs in equipping the minister of the present day. Professor Taylor followed in an address of great power, in which he referred to various criticisms passed upon our seminaries as not sending out men fitted for the times, showed how the question under discussion came back to a more fundamental question, namely, What is the aim of all theological education? and gave illustrations from his own department of work which manifested its exceedingly practical character and adaptation to the present age. He also outlined three possible plans of theological study, which might be called the medium, the minor, and the major course; the medium being the usual regular course for candidates for the ministry; the minor, a short cut for those lacking in preparation and the major, a post-graduate course for all who might wish to pursue special studies farther than the regular course would carry them. He asserted that Hartford Seminary had long felt the many disadvantages in combining the medium and minor courses, so that it had given up the minor course, and now insisted more rigidly than ever on college graduation or its equivalent as a condition of admission ; but he propounded the query whether there might not be a large field open to the Seminary in major courses which should gradually present greater and greater opportunities to those desiring to pursue special advanced studies. An informal discussion followed, the general drift of which was that there might be certain changes necessary in the common theological curriculum to adapt it to present needs, but that the great essentials should remain the same in substance, being more or less modified and adjusted in form, in order to meet present exigencies.

Francis Williams, '41, having completed fifty years of painstaking and successful ministry, the past thirty-three in a single pastorate at Chaplin, Conn., retired from active service October 1. His home will be in East Hartford, where he has purchased a house. On September 20 he preached a sermon in commemoration of the end of his half-century of ministerial work. On October 22 he and his most estimable wife will celebrate their golden wedding by a reception at their home in Chaplin.

Francis F. Williams, who lost his life in the burning of the hotel at Palmer, Mass., Aug. 3, 1891, was born at Kennebunk, Me., July 31, 1824. Mr. Williams became a Christian at an early age. He graduated from Bowdoin College in 1845, and after teaching in the South for three years, he entered Bangor Seminary. He took the last year of his theological course at East Windsor Hill, graduating in 1851. He began his ministerial service at Manchester, Conn., and was very successful. His health failed, however, and he was obliged to retire for a little while. When he resumed the active work of the ministry, he was pastor successively at Boylston, East Marshfield, Scituate, Norfolk, and Holland, Mass. He retired from his last pastorate a few years before his death, and was stopping for a time at Palmer, when he was called home.

The efficient editor of the Puget Sound department of *The Central West*, the Presbyterian organ of Nebraska and Colorado, is BENJAMIN PARSONS, '54, of Seattle, Wash.

H. W. JONES, '60, has changed his address from Vacaville to Pasadena, Cal.

A. W. FIELD, '70, has resigned his pastorate at New Marlboro, Mass.

VINCENT MOSES, '71, after four years' charge of the churches in Patten and Island Falls, Me., has resigned to accept a professorship in Lake Charles College in Louisiana.

NAHABED ABDALIAN, '77, was mistakenly reported in the Alumni Register of June as the Protestant pastor in Bardizag. He is a practicing physician at Gurun, Turkey.

V. E. LOBA, '79, has removed from Siloam Springs, Ark., to Noble, Mo. He will have charge not only of church work, but of the academy in his new field.

We clip the following from *The Presbyterian:* — "A little over a year ago the first Presbyterian church of colored people was organized in the city of Richmond, Va., with twenty members. Rev. J. E. RAWLINS, from British West Indies, a graduate of Hartford Theological Seminary, is its pastor. At its communion, July 26, four persons were received into the fellowship of the church,—three on profession of faith and one by letter. The present membership is twenty-six. There is a good Sunday-school. Ten children have been baptized since the organization. The work is connected with the Freedmen's Board, but the Presbyterian pastors of the city and their churches are also manifesting deep interest in it, and have given strong assurances of practical co-operation. The erection of a suitable place of worship is under consideration. Everything seems to give indication of a prosperous future."

T. M. PRICE, '83, has added to his list of three churches a new work at Hewitville, Minn., where a railroad station has recently been established.

During the past summer W. F. ENGLISH, '85, and his wife have been stationed at Gurun, Turkey, where they will remain at work until next April. Mr. English received the degree of Ph.D. from the University of Omaha at its last commencement.

E. W. GREENE, '85, has been elected Superintendent of Public Schools for Cache County, Utah. In this election Mr. Greene received over a thousand Mormon votes.

C. S. MILLS, '85, was installed on September 24, as pastor of the Jennings Avenue Church in Cleveland, O.

C. H. CURTIS, '86, of Portland, Oregon, was married in that city, July 10, to Miss Anna Gilt.

A remarkable religious interest is reported in the church at Upton, Mass., where A. J. DYER, '86, is pastor.

D. P. HATCH, '86, has just removed from Rockland, Me., to Paterson, N. J., where he becomes pastor of a Presbyterian church. Mr. Hatch's pastorate in Rockland has been a highly successful one, and great regret is expressed over his removal from the State of Maine.

H. H. AVERY, '87, has been compelled by ill health to close his work in St. Francis and Bird City, Kan., and to rest for a time in the hope of regaining strength.

W. A. GEORGE, '87, who has been at work at Lyndhurst, N. J., has accepted a call to the Madison Ave. (Presbyterian) Chapel in Paterson, N. J., beginning work November 1.

A. F. LYMAN, '88, is temporarily supplying the church in Abington, Mass.

H. M. LYMAN, '88, who has been for some time engaged as a civil engineer in Tennessee, goes this fall to Chicago Theological Seminary for a year of study.

RICHARD WRIGHT, '90, after supplying the pulpit at Windsor Locks, Conn., for more than a year, has accepted a call to become pastor. His installation took place on October 7, Professor Taylor preaching the sermon. Mr. Wright spent several weeks in a trip to Great Britain during the summer.

J. S. PORTER, '91, was ordained to foreign missionary work at his home church in Gilead, Conn., on September 16. Professor Bissell preached the sermon, and C. H. Barber, '80, and F. M. Hollister, '91, took part in the service. Mr. Porter soon leaves for his post in Austria under the A. B. C. F. M.

Those of the class of '91 who were not settled when our last number was issued are rapidly entering upon their work. A. L. GOLDER becomes pastor at Canton Center, Conn. CARLETON HAZEN takes charge of the church at Rochester, Vt., while J. N. PERRIN and W. S. WALKER go to Williamstown and Lunenburgh in the same State respectively.

Seminary Annals.

OPENING OF THE FIFTY-EIGHTH YEAR.

The exercises of the new Seminary year were opened on Thursday, September 17, by morning prayers. The schedule of prescribed hours went into immediate operation, so that by evening all the classes were at work. With hardly an exception all the students were on hand, and all were evidently ready for duty. Probably never in the history of the institution has the beginning of the year's work been so prompt and so energetic.

The most noticeable features of the opening were, of course, the inauguration of the elective system and the general raising of the standard of admission and of promotion. In the effort to meet the varied needs of the times and to enlarge the sphere of theological education — in which the Seminary has been prominent of recent years — the prescribed curriculum had become unwieldy. Either a reduction or a change of system was imperative. Under these conditions of necessity — the pressure of students' needs and of the developments of theological science — the elective system was adopted by the Faculty and Trustees. The prescribed course was reduced to 12 hours per week for Juniors, 10 for Middlers, and 9 for Seniors, with a requisition besides of 3 to 4 hours of elective work on Juniors, and of 5 to 6 hours on both Middlers and Seniors. The exact balance of hours and of subjects between the prescribed and the elective courses may not remain as it is. But the general timeliness of the change is shown by the facts that every one of the twenty-two electives offered for the First Semester was chosen by a larger or smaller class, and that, as soon as the schedule of hours could be arranged, the various groups of students plunged enthusiastically into their work.

In addition to the various prescribed courses in all departments, the following elective courses are now in progress : — *Professor Bissell*. The Post-Exilian Prophets (for Middlers and Seniors), Biblical Aramaic (for Middlers), Arabic (for Seniors) ; *Professor Walker*, General History, 1648–1820 (for Juniors and Middlers), Select Topics in Mediæval Church History (for Seniors) ; *Professor Beardslee*, Biblical Ecclesiology and Eschatology (for Seniors) ; *Professor Gillett*, Apologetics of the New Testament (for all classes), Historic Apologetics (for Juniors), English Philosophy (for Middlers and Seniors) ; *Professor Taylor*, Special Homiletics (for Middlers), Special Homiletics

(31)

and Evangelistics (for Seniors); *Professor Pratt*, Elementary Sight-singing (for Juniors and Middlers), Intermediate Sight-singing (for Middlers), Musical Analysis (for Middlers), Vocal Expression and Gesture (for Middlers), History and Theory of Church Music (for Seniors), Advanced Elocution (for Seniors); *Professor Perry*, Bibliographical method (for Juniors).

Among the factors in the strength of the institutional life most important is the return of President Hartranft in full vigor to his post of leadership and instruction. His entire withdrawal for ten months from active duty had been a serious crippling of the Seminary staff, and a menace to its future. His return was therefore welcomed by both teachers and students with hearty rejoicing. He at once addressed himself to supplying the gap in one side of the Systematic department left by Professor Zenos' withdrawal. The instruction in the department of New Testament exegesis has been most acceptably begun by Professor Jacobus, who has already won golden opinions from all as a man, a scholar, a teacher, and an orator. It may be doubted whether the institution ever received a new professor who so immediately proved himself perfectly at home in his position.

It was expected that the number of students would show a diminution from that of last year. Some of those then enrolled were dropped before the end of the year, some continued through only on probation, and others were evidently keeping up only with difficulty. Various providential reasons obliged a few to change their Seminary relations. The absence of President Hartranft and the withdrawal of Professors Zenos and Nash certainly diminished the apparent resources of the Faculty. The sharp emphasis put upon suitable preparation on the part of candidates for admission had the effect of turning away several. More applicants were discouraged than have been received. The result is a compact body of students, unusually homogeneous and energetic. The full roll is given on a later page. Three students undertook the entrance examinations on September 16, on the basis of which a prize scholarship was awarded to Mr. Ozora S. Davis, a graduate of Dartmouth College in 1889, and for two years Principal of the High School at White River Junction, Vt.

Among the new students it may not be improper to particularize one or two. Mr. Abé is a Japanese pastor of several years' standing, a graduate of the Doshisha, who comes here by advice of the missionaries on the field especially for the mastery of scientific methods of exegesis. Dr. Barnes, who has been for sixteen years professor in Iowa College, comes to supplement certain deficiencies in his preparation for entering ministerial work, particularly in Hebrew and in Systematic Theology. Several others come from work and experience of uncommon interest. The average age of the new-comers is over 29 years. Mr. Sleeper, who is under appointment to take charge of the musical department of Beloit College, remains part of the year for special studies in various musical subjects.

Viewed as a whole the opening of the year is felt to be highly successful. The organization of the institution's work never was more effective, the intellectual and spiritual tone of the whole fraternity never better, and the atmosphere of fellowship and good cheer never more pervasive.

ENGLISH LITERATURE PRIZE.

The Faculty of Hartford Theological Seminary take pleasure in announcing that Albert S. Cook, Ph.D., Professor of the English Language and Literature in Yale University, has authorized them to offer a prize of $50 for the best essay on " *English Literature in the Schools as an Ally of Religion*," under the following conditions : —

(1) The prize to be known as the " Hartranft Prize," in token of the donor's obligations as a student of English Literature to President Hartranft of Hartford Theological Seminary.

(2) Competition to be open to any student in the regular course of any Theological Seminary in New England.

(3) Essays to contain between 3,000 and 5,000 words.

(4) Essays to be sent to the Registrar of Hartford Theological Seminary on or before April 1, 1892, signed with a fictitious name, and accompanied by a sealed envelope inscribed with this name and containing the author's real name, together with a certificate from the Dean of his Seminary that he is a student in the regular course for the year 1891-2.

(5) The prize to be awarded by a committee of three, namely, Rev. Graham Taylor, D.D., Professor of Practical Theology in Hartford Theological Seminary, Mr. Richard E. Burton, Ph.D., of the Hartford *Courant*, and Mr. Wilbur F. Gordy, Principal of the North School, Hartford.

(6) The award to be announced and the prize paid about May 1, 1892, and all unsuccessful essays returned, if the writers desire.

(7) The successful essay to be published during the summer of 1892 in the HARTFORD SEMINARY RECORD, or some other periodical of similar grade.

ROLL OF STUDENTS FOR 1891–92.

FELLOWS.

ARTHUR L. GILLETT	appointed in 1889.
MORRIS W. MORSE	" 1890.
EDWARD E. NOURSE	" 1891.

GRADUATE STUDENT.

HENRY D. SLEEPER   Worcester, Mass.
Harvard University, ——. Hartford Seminary, 1891.

SENIOR CLASS.

HARRY G. BISSELL   Hampton, Conn.
Olivet College, 1890.

JAMES A. BLAISDELL   Beloit, Wis.
Beloit College, 1889.

IRVING A. BURNAP   Fitchburg, Mass.
Amherst College, 1888.

LYMAN P. HITCHCOCK   Hartford, Conn.
Syracuse University, 1889.

HENRY HOLMES   East Hampton, Conn.
Carleton College, ——.

ERNEST R. LATHAM   Huntsburgh, O.
Olivet College, 1888.

HENRY B. MASON   Reading, Mass.

WILLIAM J. TATE   Windsor Locks, Conn.
Trinity College, 1886.

GERHART A. WILSON   Ravenswood, Ill.
Lake Forest College, 1889.

MIDDLE CLASS.

HAIG ADADOURIAN   Adana, Turkey.
Central Turkey College, 1889.

REGINALD V. BURY   Dublin, Ireland.

LUTIE R. CORWIN   Cleveland, O.

WILLIAM A. ESTABROOK   West Dover, Vt.

HANNAH J. GILSON   Walpole, N. H.
Mt. Holyoke Seminary, 1868.

AUSTIN HAZEN, JR.   Richmond, Vt.
University of Vermont, 1885.

JOHN Q. A. JOHNSON   Nashville, Tenn.
Fisk University, 1890.

BENJAMIN W. LABAREE   Oroomiah, Persia.
Marietta College, 1888.

HAROOTUNE H. SARGAVAKIAN   Harpoot, Turkey.
Euphrates College, 1884.

NICHOLAS VAN DER PYL   Boston, Mass.

HARRY T. WILLIAMS   Moline, Ill.
Oberlin College, 1890.

JUNIOR CLASS.

ISO ABÉ — Fukuoka, Japan.
Doshisha College, 1884.

WILLARD L. BEARD — Birmingham, Conn.
Oberlin College, 1891.

THOMAS J. BELL — Altamaha, Ga.
Atlanta University, 1891.

FRANK S. BREWER — Ashton, Ill.
Beloit College, 1891.

HERBERT E. CARLETON — Hartford, Conn.
Carleton College, 1891.

OZORA S. DAVIS — White River Junction, Vt.
Dartmouth College, 1889.

DWIGHT GODDARD — Holyoke, Mass.
Worcester Polytechnic Institute, 1881.

PAUL L. LA COUR — Nashville, Tenn.
Fisk University, 1885.

JAMES A. OTIS — Irvington, Neb.
Doane College, 1891.

JAMES A. SOLANDT — Inverness, Quebec.
Oberlin College, 1891.

FREDERICK A. SUMNER — Eastford, Conn.
Oberlin College, 1891.

SPECIAL STUDENTS.

WILLIAM J. BAKER — Chicopee, Mass.
School for Christian Workers, 1891.

STEPHEN G. BARNES, PH.D., LITT.D. — Grinnell, Ia.
Lafayette College, 1873.

CURTIS M. GEER — East Windsor, Conn.
Williams College, 1887. Hartford Seminary, 1890.

WILLIAM C. HAWKS — Hartford, Conn.
Amherst College, 1885.

EDWIN M. PICKOP — Bloomfield, Conn.
Harvard University, 1884.

ALBERT H. PLUMB, JR. — Roxbury, Mass.
Amherst College, 1891.

SUMMARY.

Fellows,	-	-	-	-		3
Graduates,	-	-	-	-	-	1
Seniors,	-	-	-	-	-	9
Middlers,	-	-	-	-	-	11
Juniors,	-	-	-	-	-	11
Specials,	-	-	-	-	-	6

41

DURING THE SUMMER the members of the Faculty have not simply rested. All have made more or less special preparation for this year's instruction; some have done work of a more public character, which deserves mention. Professor Bissell has prepared a second edition of his *Hebrew Grammar* and added to it, Part III, The Syntax; has written an article on *The Pentateuchal Discussion — Present Outlook*, which appears in the September number of the *Homiletic Review* — in addition to the article in our present issue; and has printed a syllabus for work in O. T. Criticism with a chart, of his own devising, illustrating the analysis of Genesis. He also represented the Seminary at the inauguration of President Gates at Amherst, June 24, and preached the sermon at the ordination of John S. Porter, '91, as a Foreign Missionary on September 16. Professor Taylor on June 16 delivered the Commencement address before the Alumni of Rutgers College — his Alma Mater — on *The Place of Sociology in Practical Education*. At the Commencement of Dartmouth College, he gave the annual address before the Y. M. C. A. He preached the sermon at the ordination and installation of S. T. Livingston, '91, at South Egremont, Mass., on July 8; and took the same part at the installation of Richard Wright, '90, at Windsor Locks, Conn., on October 7. Professor Beardslee gave a lecture at the Summer School held at the School for Christian Workers, Springfield, Mass., on August 11; he also preached the sermon at the ordination of F. J. Perkins, '91, as a Foreign Missionary at the Presbyterian Church, Hartford, on June 16; and gave the charge to the people at the installation of T. M. Hodgdon, '88, at West Hartford on July 8. Professor Pratt completed his work as musical editor of *The Century Dictionary* in August; and read a paper before the Maine State Conference on June 18, upon *Music in Public Worship*. Professor Perry, in connection with C. S. Mills, '85, edited a new series of *The Brookfield Services* upon the Parables. Professor Gillett supplied the church at Bristol, Conn., during July and August. Professor Walker was engaged throughout the summer in special studies upon a topic in his department.

THE SUMMER WORK by students is of value both in furnishing practical experience and in revealing the need of careful preparation for future work. Not a little good is accomplished, also, in the various fields in the way of organizing new societies and in strengthening and reviving churches. The Master's work is great and the need for earnest activity is pressing. This year the geographical distribution of the work was less wide than formerly, the majority of the men laboring in the Eastern and Middle States. In New England there were 18 students. Of this number, Maine had 4; Vermont, 2; Massachusetts, 2; Connecticut, 9; Rhode Island, 1. Besides these, 4 men were employed in New York, and in Wisconsin and Kansas 1 each. It would be interesting to record how wide an influence has gone forth from the efforts made, but mere statistics do not suffice to tell the story of earnest, consecrated effort in the Master's cause.

The following is the list of students thus engaged:

H. ADADOURIAN, New York City, preaching and other work.

H. G. BISSELL, Hampton, Conn., pastoral work.

J. A. BLAISDELL, Beloit, Wis., preaching in neighboring churches.

I. A. BURNAP, Weathersfield Center, Vt., preaching.

R. V. BURY, Marlborough, Conn., pastoral work.

L. J. DAVIES, Holyoke, Mass., pastor's assistant.

W. A. ESTABROOK, West Dover and Wilmington, Vt., preaching.

A. HAZEN, JR., Middletown, Conn., preaching; no church organization.

L. P. HITCHCOCK, North Waterford, Me., preaching.

H. HOLMES, East Hampton, Conn., pastoral work.

J. Q. A. JOHNSON, Springfield, Mass., preaching.

S. V. KARMARKAR, Hartford, Conn., gave several addresses.

E. R. LATHAM, Emporia, Kan., during June and July ; Eureka, Kan., during August, preaching.

H. B. MASON, Freedom, Me., preaching.

C. D. MILLIKEN, Hartford, Conn., teaching and preaching.

A. F. NEWELL, West Woolwich, Me., preaching.

E. M. PICKOP, Bloomfield, Conn., regular pastor.

H. H. SARGAVAKIAN, Providence, R. I., work among Armenian young men.

J. S. STRONG, Rockport, Me., preaching.

W. J. TATE, Albion, Oswego Co., N. Y., preaching.

N. VAN DER PYL, Buffalo, N. Y., evangelistic work; supplied the People's Church one month.

J. E. WILDEY, Hockanum, Conn., pastoral work.

H. T. WILLIAMS. Hartford, Conn., evangelistic work.

G. A. WILSON, Hartford. Conn., during June, teaching in Brooklyn, N. Y.; during July and August, preaching.

WORK UPON the new Case Memorial Library has been pushed steadily during the summer, and the building is nearly ready for the inside finishing. The roof is almost completed, the cement floors have been laid in the stack-room, and the partitions in the second and third story of the front portion have been put up. One can now get a very satisfactory impression of the whole. The main library room is decidedly imposing, and many of the special study rooms are exceedingly attractive. A considerable time must elapse, however, before the building is ready for occupancy.

In connection with this statement in regard to the building, it may be said that work upon the books has been carried on during most of the summer. The new classification has proved a large undertaking, but is well advanced, and will undoubtedly prove of great value to all users of the Library.

A new charging system has gone into effect in the Library, which, it is hoped, will prove more efficient than the old. It is the same as that used at Amherst College. New regulations have also been printed and distributed. The Library is open, as heretofore, from 7.30 A. M. to 9.30 P. M.

THE CALENDAR for the First Semester is as follows: Sept. 17, Beginning of the Semester; Sept. 23, Informal talk by Professor Perry on *The Use of the Library;* Sept. 30 and Oct. 1, Addresses by Rev. Frank Russell, D.D., of the Evangelical Alliance on *The Religious Condition of our Communities,* and *Remedies for this Condition;* Oct. 5, School for Church Musicians opens, and Choral Union rehearsals begin; Oct. 7, Missionary Meeting, with an address by Rev. John T. Nichols on the work of the "Yale Band" in Washington; Oct. 14-16, Recess for American Board meeting; Oct. 21, Faculty Conference, led by Professor Bissell, having for its subject, *How is a wider popular knowledge of the Scriptures to be secured?* Nov. 4, Missionary Meeting; Nov. 18, Faculty Conference, led by Professor Taylor; Nov. 25-30, Thanksgiving Recess; Dec. 2, Missionary Meeting; Dec. 9, Address by Rev. W. V. W. Davis, D.D., of Worcester, Mass., on *The Influence of Classical Rhetoric upon Christian Preaching;* Dec. 16, Faculty Conference, led by Professor Pratt; Dec. 24-Jan. 4, Christmas Recess; Jan. 6, Missionary Meeting; Jan. 15 and 16, Examinations and close of the Semester.

THE REGULAR RECITATION HOURS remain as last year: at 8 A. M., 11 A. M., and 3.30 P. M., with Morning Prayers at 9.05; but the large number of electives chosen has necessitated the use of some additional hours. There is but one prescribed hour for General Exercises during the week,— on Wednesday evening at 6.30. This hour will be variously occupied, as follows: the first Wednesday in each month by a Missionary Meeting; the second by Senior preaching; the third by a Faculty Conference; and the fourth by an address from some specialist.

MORNING PRAYERS during the First Semester will be led by the Faculty in the following order: President Hartranft, who takes for his exposition *Jeremiah;* Professor Walker, *James;* Professor Bissell, *Psalms;* Professor Perry, *The Parables;* Professor Gillett, *Galatians;* Professor Beardslee, *II Kings;* Professor Pratt, selected liturgical passages of an "impressive" character; Professor Taylor, *The Words of Christ;* Professor Jacobus, *I Samuel.*

THE SERIES of addresses by specialists was very pleasantly inaugurated on September 30 and October 1, by two lectures by Rev. Frank Russell, D.D., Field Secretary of the Evangelical Alliance. After calling attention to the great religious needs of all parts of the country, he showed most conclusively that the churches were not successfully meeting those needs because of ill-distribution, lack of organization, and unconsciousness of their great mission. The remedy was found in an increasing systematic co-operation of Christian workers.

The Missionary Meeting of October 7 was addressed by Rev. John T. Nichols on the peculiar methods of organization used by the so-called "Yale Band," a company of seven Yale graduates settled in contiguous fields in Eastern Washington. He made a strong plea for the prosecution of home missionary work by similar groups of workers.

On October 9, Rev. George W. Reed, '87, who is stationed by the A. M. A. at Fort Yates, No. Dak., gave a stirring address on his work among the Indians.

AT A MEETING of the Students' Association, held October 1, the following resolution was adopted: "Inasmuch as God in His infinite wisdom has removed from our number by death our brother Mr. H. G. Papazian, we, the students of Hartford Theological Seminary hereby express our appreciation of him, as a gentleman of strong Christian character, of sweet disposition, and of manliness in his work. Deeply regretting his loss, we have assurance that this summons was but the second call of the Master, 'Follow thou me.' "

ON THE EVENING of Friday, October 2, the Faculty gave a reception to the students, the resident Trustees, and the ladies of the Women's Advisory Committee. The Chapel and one of the adjoining rooms were thrown open and very tastefully decorated. President Hartranft and Miss Ida Berg received, and Miss Cooley and Miss Allen presided at the refreshment table. The occasion proved highly enjoyable to all who participated.

THE CHORAL UNION is already well launched on its twelfth season. Its work is being prosecuted, as last year, by means of two choruses, the larger for the broad effects of oratorio music, and the smaller for part-singing and the niceties of expression. The former meets on Monday evenings, and the latter on Wednesday. The conductorship of the Large Chorus, which a year ago was to have devolved upon Mr. Homer A. Norris of Boston, but which he was prevented from taking on account of a sudden and serious illness, was not permanently filled until July. It will be remembered that during last year this chorus was under the care first of Professor Pratt and then of Mr. John S. Camp, who kindly volunteered to serve *ad interim*. In July the directors unanimously chose Mr. Richmond P. Paine, of New Britain, the permanent conductor. Mr. Paine is making a specialty of chorus singing and is rapidly winning a reputation throughout New England in that department. Under his leadership the chorus promises to regain the size and efficiency of some years ago. The opening rehearsals have been well attended and marked with much enthusiasm. The works now in preparation are Mendelssohn's great oratorio, "St. Paul," and Sir Arthur Sullivan's "Golden Legend," a brilliant modern setting of Longfellow's well-known poem. Neither of these works has been sung in Hartford. The list of subscribers to the next May Festival is already well under way, and important negotiations for orchestra and soloists are pending.

The Small Chorus is again under the care of Mr. E. N. Anderson, of Worcester, the popular vocal teacher in the School for Church Musicians. Its membership is limited to experienced singers. The works now in rehearsal comprise the unfinished "Christus" of Mendelssohn, with selected part-songs by Rhineberger, Cowen, and others. It is probable that a musicale will be given in December.

THE SCHOOL FOR CHURCH MUSICIANS enters upon its second year under favorable auspices. Not only is it formally recognized by the Trustees of the Seminary as an appendix to the Seminary apparatus and cèrtain privileges accorded to it thus, but it is backed by a special financial guaranty furnished by a company of interested gentlemen and ladies, mostly in Hartford. Its circular announcement gives the following list of instructors:

E. N. ANDERSON, Vocal Culture and Interpretation.
Conductor of the Small Chorus of the Choral Union.

EDWARD D. HALE, Piano-Playing, Advanced and Elementary.
Professor in the New England Conservatory, Boston.

WILLIAM C. HAMMOND, Organ-Playing.
Organist, Holyoke, and Professor, Smith College.

MRS. VIRGINIA P. MARWICK, Vocal Culture.
Church and Concert Singer.

HOMER A. NORRIS, Composition, including Harmony, Counterpoint and Orchestration. Organ-Playing.
Organist, Boston. Pupil of Dubois and Guilmant.

RICHMOND P. PAINE.
Conductor of the Large Chorus of the Choral Union.

WALDO S. PRATT, History and Science.
Professor, Hartford Theological Seminary.

HENRY DIKE SLEEPER, Sight-Reading, Harmony and Counterpoint.
Professor-elect, Beloit College.

It will be seen that this list fully sustains the high standard of ability that was set last year. The advantages offered are evidently beginning to be understood, and the lists of special pupils are steadily filling up.

The managers of the School have decided to hold the plans for a regular three-years' course of study somewhat in abeyance until other work is better established. Their efforts have been much assisted by the kind permission extended by the South Baptist Church for the use, at least for the present, of their fine three-manual organ for lessons.

AS THIS ISSUE goes to press, arrangements are being perfected for an elaborate series of "University Extension" lectures and classes under the leadership of the Seminary Faculty. The list of instructors already secured includes the following names: — Rev. S. J. Andrews, D.D., Professor S. G. Barnes, Ph.D., Professor C. S. Beardslee, Miss Margaret Blythe, Mr. Richard E. Burton, Ph.D., Mr. Frederick H. Chapin, Mr. Edward D. Hale, Mr. Frederick B. Hartranft, Rev. E. H. Knight, Rev. E. P. Parker, D.D., Hon. Nathaniel Shipman, LL.D., Melancthon Storrs, M.D., and Professor Graham Taylor, D.D.

Exhaustion

Horsford's Acid Phosphate

Prepared under the direction of Prof. E. N. Horsford.

Every fibre of the human body contains the phosphates. They are the vital elements of every tissue, and are essential to the maintenance and promotion of sound bodily health.

These phosphates are ·consumed with every effort, and if the waste is not supplied exhaustion will follow.

Horsford's Acid Phosphate supplies these phosphates, and thereby relieves exhaustion and increases the capacity for labor.

Dr. A. N. Krout, Van Wert, O., says:

"Decidedly beneficial in nervous exhaustion."

Dr. S. T. Newman, St. Louis, Mo., says:

"A remedy of great service in many forms of exhaustion."

Dr. Gustave A. Shane, Steubenville, O., says:

"Especially gratifying benefit in its use in nervous irritability and exhaustion, dependent upon digestive derangements."

Descriptive pamphlet free on application to

Rumford Chemical Works, Providence, R. I.

Beware of Substitutes and Imitations.

CAUTION.— Be sure the word "Horsford's is <u>printed</u> on the label. All others are spurious. Never sold in bulk.

STORRS & CANDEE,

THE GENESIS OF GENESIS.

A STUDY OF THE DOCUMENTARY SOURCES OF THE FIRST BOOK OF
MOSES IN ACCORDANCE WITH THE RESULTS OF CRITICAL
SCIENCE ILLUSTRATED IN THE PRESENCE OF
BIBLES WITHIN THE BIBLE,

By Benjamin Wisner Bacon.

The work consists of three parts, in the first of which the methods of the higher criticism are explained and illustrated ; in the second part the results are laid before the reader, and in the third part critical notes are added. There will be an introduction by Prof. Geo. F. Moore of Andover Theological Seminary.

This work will furnish the reader with information compactly presented, that can only be gleaned by a wide range of reading. It will be issued in the coming autumn by

THE STUDENT PUBLISHING CO.,
HARTFORD, CONN.

www.ingramcontent.com/pod-product-compliance
Lightning Source LLC
Chambersburg PA
CBHW031817090426

42739CB00008B/1313